MY PET
BALL PYTHON LOGBOOK

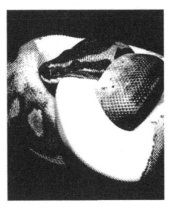

THIS BOOK BELONGS TO:

MY PET
BALL PYTHON LOGBOOK

ALL ABOUT YOUR SNAKE

PHOTO/DRAWING

NAME:

DOB:

SPECIES:

SEX:

COLOR & MARKING:

LINCENSE #:

ADOPTION PLACE:

MORPH:

MICROCHIP:

HOW WE MET:

HOW HE/HER GOT NAME:

OWNER'S INFORMATION

NAME:

ADDRESS:

PHONE: EMAIL:

VET INFORMATION

CLINIC: VET:

ADDRESS:

PHONE: EMAIL:

IMPORTANT NUMBERS

NAME:	PHONE:	ADDRESS:

NOTES:

MEDICATION RECORD/VET VISITS

DATE: REASON FOR VISIT: NEXT VISIT:

DATE: REASON FOR VISIT: NEXT VISIT:

DATE: REASON FOR VISIT: NEXT VISIT:

DATE: REASON FOR VISIT: NEXT VISIT:

DATE: REASON FOR VISIT: NEXT VISIT:

DATE: REASON FOR VISIT: NEXT VISIT:

DATE: REASON FOR VISIT: NEXT VISIT:

MEDICATION

MEDICATION:	DATE:	NOTES:

WEIGHT TRACKER

DATE	WEIGHT BEFORE	CURRENT WEIGHT	+/-

WEIGHT TRACKER

DATE	WEIGHT BEFORE	CURRENT WEIGHT	+/-

SHED TRACKER

DATE SHED:	GOOD SHED		NOTES:
	Y	N	
	Y	N	
	Y	N	
	Y	N	
	Y	N	
	Y	N	
	Y	N	
	Y	N	
	Y	N	
	Y	N	
	Y	N	
	Y	N	
	Y	N	
	Y	N	
	Y	N	
	Y	N	
	Y	N	
	Y	N	
	Y	N	
	Y	N	

EXPENSES

DATE:	SOURCE	DESCRIPTION:	AMOUNT:

EXPENSES

DATE:	SOURCE	DESCRIPTION:	AMOUNT:

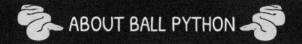 ABOUT BALL PYTHON

 life span

- Up to 30 years

 Size

- 4-5 feet long

 Diet

- Carnivore

 Minimum Habitat Size

- 40+ gallons for adults

Daily, Weekly & Monthly Activity Guide

Daily Activity

 Clean and refresh water bowl

 Check temperatures

 Check humidity

 Spot clean any waste

 Remove any skin shed

 Visual inspect

Weekly Activity

 Feed Snake

 Clean glass

 Top up substrate

 Clean any decorative wood, plants etc

 Physically inspect Snake

 Weigh and record

Monthly Activity

 Remove and replace all substrate

DAILY CHECKLIST

Activity	WEEK OF	SUN	MON	TUE	WED	THU	FRI	SAT
Clean and refresh water bowl		☐	☐	☐	☐	☐	☐	☐
Check temperatures		☐	☐	☐	☐	☐	☐	☐
Check humidity		☐	☐	☐	☐	☐	☐	☐
Spot clean any waste		☐	☐	☐	☐	☐	☐	☐
Remove any skin shed		☐	☐	☐	☐	☐	☐	☐
Visual inspect		☐	☐	☐	☐	☐	☐	☐

NOTES:

WEEKLY, MONTHLY CHECKLIST

WEEKLY ACTIVITY   DATE:

- ☐ Feed Snake
- ☐ Clean glass
- ☐ Top up substrate
- ☐ Clean any decorative wood, plants etc
- ☐ Physically inspect Snake
- ☐ Weigh and record

MONTHLY ACTIVITY   DATE:

- ☐ Remove and replace all substrate

HEALTH CHECKLIST   DATE:

- ☐Y ☐N Active and alert
- ☐Y ☐N Clear eyes (except when shedding)
- ☐Y ☐N Eats regularly
- ☐Y ☐N Good body composition
- ☐Y ☐N Healthy, supple, smooth skin
- ☐Y ☐N Regularly sheds skin in one complete piece
- ☐Y ☐N Free of mites and ticks

NOTES:

HIGHLIGHT OF THE WEEK:

DAILY CHECKLIST

Activity	WEEK OF						
	SUN	MON	TUE	WED	THU	FRI	SAT
Clean and refresh water bowl	☐	☐	☐	☐	☐	☐	☐
Check temperatures	☐	☐	☐	☐	☐	☐	☐
Check humidity	☐	☐	☐	☐	☐	☐	☐
Spot clean any waste	☐	☐	☐	☐	☐	☐	☐
Remove any skin shed	☐	☐	☐	☐	☐	☐	☐
Visual inspect	☐	☐	☐	☐	☐	☐	☐

NOTES:

WEEKLY, MONTHLY CHECKLIST

WEEKLY ACTIVITY   DATE: _____

- ☐ Feed Snake _____
- ☐ Clean glass
- ☐ Top up substrate
- ☐ Clean any decorative wood, plants etc
- ☐ Physically inspect Snake
- ☐ Weigh and record

MONTHLY ACTIVITY   DATE: _____

- ☐ Remove and replace all substrate

HEALTH CHECKLIST   DATE: _____

- ☐ ☐ Active and alert
- ☐ ☐ Clear eyes (except when shedding)
- ☐ ☐ Eats regularly
- ☐ ☐ Good body composition
- ☐ ☐ Healthy, supple, smooth skin
- ☐ ☐ Regularly sheds skin in one complete piece
- ☐ ☐ Free of mites and ticks

NOTES:

HIGHLIGHT OF THE WEEK:

DAILY CHECKLIST

Activity	WEEK OF						
	SUN	MON	TUE	WED	THU	FRI	SAT
Clean and refresh water bowl	☐	☐	☐	☐	☐	☐	☐
Check temperatures	☐	☐	☐	☐	☐	☐	☐
Check humidity	☐	☐	☐	☐	☐	☐	☐
Spot clean any waste	☐	☐	☐	☐	☐	☐	☐
Remove any skin shed	☐	☐	☐	☐	☐	☐	☐
Visual inspect	☐	☐	☐	☐	☐	☐	☐

NOTES:

WEEKLY, MONTHLY CHECKLIST

WEEKLY ACTIVITY   DATE:

- [ ] Feed Snake
- [ ] Clean glass
- [ ] Top up substrate
- [ ] Clean any decorative wood, plants etc
- [ ] Physically inspect Snake
- [ ] Weigh and record

MONTHLY ACTIVITY   DATE:

- [ ] Remove and replace all substrate

HEALTH CHECKLIST   DATE:

- [ ] Y [ ] N   Active and alert
- [ ] Y [ ] N   Clear eyes (except when shedding)
- [ ] Y [ ] N   Eats regularly
- [ ] Y [ ] N   Good body composition
- [ ] Y [ ] N   Healthy, supple, smooth skin
- [ ] Y [ ] N   Regularly sheds skin in one complete piece
- [ ] Y [ ] N   Free of mites and ticks

NOTES:

HIGHLIGHT OF THE WEEK:

DAILY CHECKLIST

📅 Activity	WEEK OF						
	SUN	MON	TUE	WED	THU	FRI	SAT
Clean and refresh water bowl	☐	☐	☐	☐	☐	☐	☐
Check temperatures	☐	☐	☐	☐	☐	☐	☐
Check humidity	☐	☐	☐	☐	☐	☐	☐
Spot clean any waste	☐	☐	☐	☐	☐	☐	☐
Remove any skin shed	☐	☐	☐	☐	☐	☐	☐
Visual inspect	☐	☐	☐	☐	☐	☐	☐

NOTES:

WEEKLY, MONTHLY CHECKLIST

WEEKLY ACTIVITY DATE:

- [ ] Feed Snake
- [ ] Clean glass
- [ ] Top up substrate
- [ ] Clean any decorative wood, plants etc
- [ ] Physically inspect Snake
- [ ] Weigh and record

MONTHLY ACTIVITY DATE:

- [ ] Remove and replace all substrate

HEALTH CHECKLIST DATE:

- [ ] Y [ ] N Active and alert
- [ ] Y [ ] N Clear eyes (except when shedding)
- [ ] Y [ ] N Eats regularly
- [ ] Y [ ] N Good body composition
- [ ] Y [ ] N Healthy, supple, smooth skin
- [ ] Y [ ] N Regularly sheds skin in one complete piece
- [ ] Y [ ] N Free of mites and ticks

NOTES:

HIGHLIGHT OF THE WEEK:

DAILY CHECKLIST

Activity	WEEK OF						
	SUN	MON	TUE	WED	THU	FRI	SAT
Clean and refresh water bowl	☐	☐	☐	☐	☐	☐	☐
Check temperatures	☐	☐	☐	☐	☐	☐	☐
Check humidity	☐	☐	☐	☐	☐	☐	☐
Spot clean any waste	☐	☐	☐	☐	☐	☐	☐
Remove any skin shed	☐	☐	☐	☐	☐	☐	☐
Visual inspect	☐	☐	☐	☐	☐	☐	☐

NOTES:

WEEKLY, MONTHLY CHECKLIST

WEEKLY ACTIVITY   DATE: _____

- [ ] Feed Snake _____
- [ ] Clean glass
- [ ] Top up substrate
- [ ] Clean any decorative wood, plants etc
- [ ] Physically inspect Snake
- [ ] Weigh and record

_____

MONTHLY ACTIVITY   DATE: _____

- [ ] Remove and replace all substrate

HEALTH CHECKLIST   DATE: _____

- [ ] Y [ ] Active and alert
- [ ] Y [ ] Clear eyes (except when shedding)
- [ ] Y [ ] Eats regularly
- [ ] [ ] Good body composition
- [ ] Y [ ] Healthy, supple, smooth skin
- [ ] Y [ ] Regularly sheds skin in one complete piece
- [ ] Y [ ] Free of mites and ticks

NOTES:

HIGHLIGHT OF THE WEEK:

DAILY CHECKLIST

Activity	WEEK OF						
	SUN	MON	TUE	WED	THU	FRI	SAT
Clean and refresh water bowl	☐	☐	☐	☐	☐	☐	☐
Check temperatures	☐	☐	☐	☐	☐	☐	☐
Check humidity	☐	☐	☐	☐	☐	☐	☐
Spot clean any waste	☐	☐	☐	☐	☐	☐	☐
Remove any skin shed	☐	☐	☐	☐	☐	☐	☐
Visual inspect	☐	☐	☐	☐	☐	☐	☐

NOTES:

WEEKLY, MONTHLY CHECKLIST

WEEKLY ACTIVITY   DATE:

- [ ] Feed Snake
- [ ] Clean glass
- [ ] Top up substrate
- [ ] Clean any decorative wood, plants etc
- [ ] Physically inspect Snake
- [ ] Weigh and record

MONTHLY ACTIVITY   DATE:

- [ ] Remove and replace all substrate

HEALTH CHECKLIST   DATE:

- [ ] Y [ ] N Active and alert
- [ ] Y [ ] N Clear eyes (except when shedding)
- [ ] Y [ ] N Eats regularly
- [ ] Y [ ] N Good body composition
- [ ] Y [ ] N Healthy, supple, smooth skin
- [ ] Y [ ] N Regularly sheds skin in one complete piece
- [ ] Y [ ] N Free of mites and ticks

NOTES:

HIGHLIGHT OF THE WEEK:

DAILY CHECKLIST

Activity	WEEK OF	SUN	MON	TUE	WED	THU	FRI	SAT
Clean and refresh water bowl		☐	☐	☐	☐	☐	☐	☐
Check temperatures		☐	☐	☐	☐	☐	☐	☐
Check humidity		☐	☐	☐	☐	☐	☐	☐
Spot clean any waste		☐	☐	☐	☐	☐	☐	☐
Remove any skin shed		☐	☐	☐	☐	☐	☐	☐
Visual inspect		☐	☐	☐	☐	☐	☐	☐

NOTES:

WEEKLY, MONTHLY CHECKLIST

WEEKLY ACTIVITY   DATE:

- [ ] Feed Snake
- [ ] Clean glass
- [ ] Top up substrate
- [ ] Clean any decorative wood, plants etc
- [ ] Physically inspect Snake
- [ ] Weigh and record

MONTHLY ACTIVITY   DATE:

- [ ] Remove and replace all substrate

HEALTH CHECKLIST   DATE:

Y	N	
☐	☐	Active and alert
☐	☐	Clear eyes (except when shedding)
☐	☐	Eats regularly
☐	☐	Good body composition
☐	☐	Healthy, supple, smooth skin
☐	☐	Regularly sheds skin in one complete piece
☐	☐	Free of mites and ticks

NOTES:

HIGHLIGHT OF THE WEEK:

DAILY CHECKLIST

Activity	WEEK OF						
	SUN	MON	TUE	WED	THU	FRI	SAT
Clean and refresh water bowl	☐	☐	☐	☐	☐	☐	☐
Check temperatures	☐	☐	☐	☐	☐	☐	☐
Check humidity	☐	☐	☐	☐	☐	☐	☐
Spot clean any waste	☐	☐	☐	☐	☐	☐	☐
Remove any skin shed	☐	☐	☐	☐	☐	☐	☐
Visual inspect	☐	☐	☐	☐	☐	☐	☐

NOTES:

WEEKLY, MONTHLY CHECKLIST

WEEKLY ACTIVITY   DATE: [   ]

- ☐ Feed Snake [   ]
- ☐ Clean glass
- ☐ Top up substrate
- ☐ Clean any decorative wood, plants etc
- ☐ Physically inspect Snake
- ☐ Weigh and record

[   ]

MONTHLY ACTIVITY   DATE: [   ]

- ☐ Remove and replace all substrate

HEALTH CHECKLIST   DATE: [   ]

- Y ☐ N ☐ Active and alert
- Y ☐ N ☐ Clear eyes (except when shedding)
- Y ☐ N ☐ Eats regularly
- ☐ ☐ Good body composition
- Y ☐ N ☐ Healthy, supple, smooth skin
- ☐ ☐ Regularly sheds skin in one complete piece
- Y ☐ N ☐ Free of mites and ticks

NOTES:

[   ]

HIGHLIGHT OF THE WEEK:

DAILY CHECKLIST

Activity	WEEK OF						
	SUN	MON	TUE	WED	THU	FRI	SAT
Clean and refresh water bowl	☐	☐	☐	☐	☐	☐	☐
Check temperatures	☐	☐	☐	☐	☐	☐	☐
Check humidity	☐	☐	☐	☐	☐	☐	☐
Spot clean any waste	☐	☐	☐	☐	☐	☐	☐
Remove any skin shed	☐	☐	☐	☐	☐	☐	☐
Visual inspect	☐	☐	☐	☐	☐	☐	☐

NOTES:

WEEKLY, MONTHLY CHECKLIST

WEEKLY ACTIVITY   DATE:

- [ ] Feed Snake
- [ ] Clean glass
- [ ] Top up substrate
- [ ] Clean any decorative wood, plants etc
- [ ] Physically inspect Snake
- [ ] Weigh and record

MONTHLY ACTIVITY   DATE:

- [ ] Remove and replace all substrate

HEALTH CHECKLIST   DATE:

- [Y] [N] Active and alert
- [Y] [N] Clear eyes (except when shedding)
- [Y] [N] Eats regularly
- [Y] [N] Good body composition
- [Y] [N] Healthy, supple, smooth skin
- [Y] [N] Regularly sheds skin in one complete piece
- [Y] [N] Free of mites and ticks

NOTES:

HIGHLIGHT OF THE WEEK:

DAILY CHECKLIST

Activity	WEEK OF						
	SUN	MON	TUE	WED	THU	FRI	SAT
Clean and refresh water bowl	☐	☐	☐	☐	☐	☐	☐
Check temperatures	☐	☐	☐	☐	☐	☐	☐
Check humidity	☐	☐	☐	☐	☐	☐	☐
Spot clean any waste	☐	☐	☐	☐	☐	☐	☐
Remove any skin shed	☐	☐	☐	☐	☐	☐	☐
Visual inspect	☐	☐	☐	☐	☐	☐	☐

NOTES:

WEEKLY, MONTHLY CHECKLIST

WEEKLY ACTIVITY   DATE:

- ☐ Feed Snake _____
- ☐ Clean glass
- ☐ Top up substrate
- ☐ Clean any decorative wood, plants etc
- ☐ Physically inspect Snake
- ☐ Weigh and record

MONTHLY ACTIVITY   DATE:

- ☐ Remove and replace all substrate

HEALTH CHECKLIST   DATE:

- ☐Y ☐N Active and alert
- ☐Y ☐N Clear eyes (except when shedding)
- ☐Y ☐N Eats regularly
- ☐Y ☐N Good body composition
- ☐Y ☐N Healthy, supple, smooth skin
- ☐Y ☐N Regularly sheds skin in one complete piece
- ☐Y ☐N Free of mites and ticks

NOTES:

HIGHLIGHT OF THE WEEK:

DAILY CHECKLIST

Activity	WEEK OF	SUN	MON	TUE	WED	THU	FRI	SAT
Clean and refresh water bowl		☐	☐	☐	☐	☐	☐	☐
Check temperatures		☐	☐	☐	☐	☐	☐	☐
Check humidity		☐	☐	☐	☐	☐	☐	☐
Spot clean any waste		☐	☐	☐	☐	☐	☐	☐
Remove any skin shed		☐	☐	☐	☐	☐	☐	☐
Visual inspect		☐	☐	☐	☐	☐	☐	☐

NOTES:

WEEKLY, MONTHLY CHECKLIST

WEEKLY ACTIVITY   DATE:

- [ ] Feed Snake
- [ ] Clean glass
- [ ] Top up substrate
- [ ] Clean any decorative wood, plants etc
- [ ] Physically inspect Snake
- [ ] Weigh and record

MONTHLY ACTIVITY   DATE:

- [ ] Remove and replace all substrate

HEALTH CHECKLIST   DATE:

- [ ] [ ] Active and alert
- [ ] [ ] Clear eyes (except when shedding)
- [ ] [ ] Eats regularly
- [ ] [ ] Good body composition
- [ ] [ ] Healthy, supple, smooth skin
- [ ] [ ] Regularly sheds skin in one complete piece
- [ ] [ ] Free of mites and ticks

NOTES:

HIGHLIGHT OF THE WEEK:

DAILY CHECKLIST

Activity	WEEK OF						
	SUN	MON	TUE	WED	THU	FRI	SAT
Clean and refresh water bowl	☐	☐	☐	☐	☐	☐	☐
Check temperatures	☐	☐	☐	☐	☐	☐	☐
Check humidity	☐	☐	☐	☐	☐	☐	☐
Spot clean any waste	☐	☐	☐	☐	☐	☐	☐
Remove any skin shed	☐	☐	☐	☐	☐	☐	☐
Visual inspect	☐	☐	☐	☐	☐	☐	☐

NOTES:

WEEKLY, MONTHLY CHECKLIST

WEEKLY ACTIVITY   DATE: _____

- [ ] Feed Snake _____
- [ ] Clean glass
- [ ] Top up substrate
- [ ] Clean any decorative wood, plants etc
- [ ] Physically inspect Snake
- [ ] Weigh and record

_____

MONTHLY ACTIVITY   DATE: _____

- [ ] Remove and replace all substrate

HEALTH CHECKLIST   DATE: _____

Y	N	
☐	☐	Active and alert
☐	☐	Clear eyes (except when shedding)
☐	☐	Eats regularly
☐	☐	Good body composition
☐	☐	Healthy, supple, smooth skin
☐	☐	Regularly sheds skin in one complete piece
☐	☐	Free of mites and ticks

NOTES:

HIGHLIGHT OF THE WEEK:

DAILY CHECKLIST

📅 Activity	WEEK OF

		SUN	MON	TUE	WED	THU	FRI	SAT
	Clean and refresh water bowl	☐	☐	☐	☐	☐	☐	☐
	Check temperatures	☐	☐	☐	☐	☐	☐	☐
	Check humidity	☐	☐	☐	☐	☐	☐	☐
	Spot clean any waste	☐	☐	☐	☐	☐	☐	☐
	Remove any skin shed	☐	☐	☐	☐	☐	☐	☐
	Visual inspect	☐	☐	☐	☐	☐	☐	☐

NOTES:

WEEKLY, MONTHLY CHECKLIST

WEEKLY ACTIVITY   DATE:

☐ Feed Snake

☐ Clean glass

☐ Top up substrate

☐ Clean any decorative wood, plants etc

☐ Physically inspect Snake

☐ Weigh and record

MONTHLY ACTIVITY   DATE:

☐ Remove and replace all substrate

HEALTH CHECKLIST   DATE:

☐Y ☐N Active and alert

☐Y ☐N Clear eyes (except when shedding)

☐Y ☐N Eats regularly

☐Y ☐N Good body composition

☐Y ☐N Healthy, supple, smooth skin

☐Y ☐N Regularly sheds skin in one complete piece

☐Y ☐N Free of mites and ticks

NOTES:

HIGHLIGHT OF THE WEEK:

DAILY CHECKLIST

Activity	WEEK OF	SUN	MON	TUE	WED	THU	FRI	SAT
Clean and refresh water bowl		☐	☐	☐	☐	☐	☐	☐
Check temperatures		☐	☐	☐	☐	☐	☐	☐
Check humidity		☐	☐	☐	☐	☐	☐	☐
Spot clean any waste		☐	☐	☐	☐	☐	☐	☐
Remove any skin shed		☐	☐	☐	☐	☐	☐	☐
Visual inspect		☐	☐	☐	☐	☐	☐	☐

NOTES:

WEEKLY, MONTHLY CHECKLIST

WEEKLY ACTIVITY   DATE:

- [ ] Feed Snake
- [ ] Clean glass
- [ ] Top up substrate
- [ ] Clean any decorative wood, plants etc
- [ ] Physically inspect Snake
- [ ] Weigh and record

MONTHLY ACTIVITY   DATE:

- [ ] Remove and replace all substrate

HEALTH CHECKLIST   DATE:

- [ ] Y [ ] N Active and alert
- [ ] Y [ ] N Clear eyes (except when shedding)
- [ ] Y [ ] N Eats regularly
- [ ] Y [ ] N Good body composition
- [ ] Y [ ] N Healthy, supple, smooth skin
- [ ] Y [ ] N Regularly sheds skin in one complete piece
- [ ] Y [ ] N Free of mites and ticks

NOTES:

HIGHLIGHT OF THE WEEK:

DAILY CHECKLIST

Activity	WEEK OF						
	SUN	MON	TUE	WED	THU	FRI	SAT
Clean and refresh water bowl	☐	☐	☐	☐	☐	☐	☐
Check temperatures	☐	☐	☐	☐	☐	☐	☐
Check humidity	☐	☐	☐	☐	☐	☐	☐
Spot clean any waste	☐	☐	☐	☐	☐	☐	☐
Remove any skin shed	☐	☐	☐	☐	☐	☐	☐
Visual inspect	☐	☐	☐	☐	☐	☐	☐

NOTES:

WEEKLY, MONTHLY CHECKLIST

WEEKLY ACTIVITY   DATE: [   ]

- ☐ Feed Snake [   ]
- ☐ Clean glass
- ☐ Top up substrate
- ☐ Clean any decorative wood, plants etc
- ☐ Physically inspect Snake
- ☐ Weigh and record

[   ]

MONTHLY ACTIVITY   DATE: [   ]

- ☐ Remove and replace all substrate

HEALTH CHECKLIST   DATE: [   ]

- ☐Y ☐N Active and alert
- ☐Y ☐N Clear eyes (except when shedding)
- ☐Y ☐N Eats regularly
- ☐Y ☐N Good body composition
- ☐Y ☐N Healthy, supple, smooth skin
- ☐Y ☐N Regularly sheds skin in one complete piece
- ☐Y ☐N Free of mites and ticks

NOTES:

HIGHLIGHT OF THE WEEK:

DAILY CHECKLIST

Activity	WEEK OF						
	SUN	MON	TUE	WED	THU	FRI	SAT
Clean and refresh water bowl	☐	☐	☐	☐	☐	☐	☐
Check temperatures	☐	☐	☐	☐	☐	☐	☐
Check humidity	☐	☐	☐	☐	☐	☐	☐
Spot clean any waste	☐	☐	☐	☐	☐	☐	☐
Remove any skin shed	☐	☐	☐	☐	☐	☐	☐
Visual inspect	☐	☐	☐	☐	☐	☐	☐

NOTES:

WEEKLY, MONTHLY CHECKLIST

WEEKLY ACTIVITY   DATE:

- [ ] Feed Snake
- [ ] Clean glass
- [ ] Top up substrate
- [ ] Clean any decorative wood, plants etc
- [ ] Physically inspect Snake
- [ ] Weigh and record

MONTHLY ACTIVITY   DATE:

- [ ] Remove and replace all substrate

HEALTH CHECKLIST   DATE:

- Y N Active and alert
- Y N Clear eyes (except when shedding)
- Y N Eats regularly
- Y N Good body composition
- Y N Healthy, supple, smooth skin
- Y N Regularly sheds skin in one complete piece
- Y N Free of mites and ticks

NOTES:

HIGHLIGHT OF THE WEEK:

DAILY CHECKLIST

Activity	WEEK OF						
	SUN	MON	TUE	WED	THU	FRI	SAT
Clean and refresh water bowl	☐	☐	☐	☐	☐	☐	☐
Check temperatures	☐	☐	☐	☐	☐	☐	☐
Check humidity	☐	☐	☐	☐	☐	☐	☐
Spot clean any waste	☐	☐	☐	☐	☐	☐	☐
Remove any skin shed	☐	☐	☐	☐	☐	☐	☐
Visual inspect	☐	☐	☐	☐	☐	☐	☐

NOTES:

WEEKLY, MONTHLY CHECKLIST

WEEKLY ACTIVITY   DATE: _____

- [ ] Feed Snake _____
- [ ] Clean glass
- [ ] Top up substrate
- [ ] Clean any decorative wood, plants etc
- [ ] Physically inspect Snake
- [ ] Weigh and record

_____

MONTHLY ACTIVITY   DATE: _____

- [ ] Remove and replace all substrate

HEALTH CHECKLIST   DATE: _____

- [ ] Y [ ] N Active and alert
- [ ] Y [ ] N Clear eyes (except when shedding)
- [ ] Y [ ] N Eats regularly
- [ ] Y [ ] N Good body composition
- [ ] Y [ ] N Healthy, supple, smooth skin
- [ ] Y [ ] N Regularly sheds skin in one complete piece
- [ ] Y [ ] N Free of mites and ticks

NOTES:

HIGHLIGHT OF THE WEEK:

DAILY CHECKLIST

Activity	WEEK OF						
	SUN	MON	TUE	WED	THU	FRI	SAT
Clean and refresh water bowl	☐	☐	☐	☐	☐	☐	☐
Check temperatures	☐	☐	☐	☐	☐	☐	☐
Check humidity	☐	☐	☐	☐	☐	☐	☐
Spot clean any waste	☐	☐	☐	☐	☐	☐	☐
Remove any skin shed	☐	☐	☐	☐	☐	☐	☐
Visual inspect	☐	☐	☐	☐	☐	☐	☐

NOTES:

WEEKLY, MONTHLY CHECKLIST

WEEKLY ACTIVITY   DATE: [ ]

- ☐ Feed Snake [ ]
- ☐ Clean glass
- ☐ Top up substrate
- ☐ Clean any decorative wood, plants etc
- ☐ Physically inspect Snake
- ☐ Weigh and record

[ ]

MONTHLY ACTIVITY   DATE: [ ]

- ☐ Remove and replace all substrate

HEALTH CHECKLIST   DATE: [ ]

- ☐Y ☐N Active and alert
- ☐Y ☐N Clear eyes (except when shedding)
- ☐Y ☐N Eats regularly
- ☐Y ☐N Good body composition
- ☐Y ☐N Healthy, supple, smooth skin
- ☐Y ☐N Regularly sheds skin in one complete piece
- ☐Y ☐N Free of mites and ticks

NOTES:

HIGHLIGHT OF THE WEEK:

DAILY CHECKLIST

Activity	WEEK OF						
	SUN	MON	TUE	WED	THU	FRI	SAT
Clean and refresh water bowl	☐	☐	☐	☐	☐	☐	☐
Check temperatures	☐	☐	☐	☐	☐	☐	☐
Check humidity	☐	☐	☐	☐	☐	☐	☐
Spot clean any waste	☐	☐	☐	☐	☐	☐	☐
Remove any skin shed	☐	☐	☐	☐	☐	☐	☐
Visual inspect	☐	☐	☐	☐	☐	☐	☐

NOTES:

WEEKLY, MONTHLY CHECKLIST

WEEKLY ACTIVITY   DATE: [   ]

- [ ] Feed Snake [   ]
- [ ] Clean glass
- [ ] Top up substrate
- [ ] Clean any decorative wood, plants etc
- [ ] Physically inspect Snake
- [ ] Weigh and record

[   ]

MONTHLY ACTIVITY   DATE: [   ]

- [ ] Remove and replace all substrate

HEALTH CHECKLIST   DATE: [   ]

- [Y] [N] Active and alert
- [Y] [N] Clear eyes (except when shedding)
- [Y] [N] Eats regularly
- [Y] [N] Good body composition
- [Y] [N] Healthy, supple, smooth skin
- [Y] [N] Regularly sheds skin in one complete piece
- [Y] [N] Free of mites and ticks

NOTES:

HIGHLIGHT OF THE WEEK:

DAILY CHECKLIST

Activity	WEEK OF						
	SUN	MON	TUE	WED	THU	FRI	SAT
Clean and refresh water bowl	☐	☐	☐	☐	☐	☐	☐
Check temperatures	☐	☐	☐	☐	☐	☐	☐
Check humidity	☐	☐	☐	☐	☐	☐	☐
Spot clean any waste	☐	☐	☐	☐	☐	☐	☐
Remove any skin shed	☐	☐	☐	☐	☐	☐	☐
Visual inspect	☐	☐	☐	☐	☐	☐	☐

NOTES:

WEEKLY, MONTHLY CHECKLIST

WEEKLY ACTIVITY   DATE: _____

- [ ] Feed Snake _____
- [ ] Clean glass
- [ ] Top up substrate
- [ ] Clean any decorative wood, plants etc
- [ ] Physically inspect Snake
- [ ] Weigh and record

_____

MONTHLY ACTIVITY   DATE: _____

- [ ] Remove and replace all substrate

HEALTH CHECKLIST   DATE: _____

- [ ] Y [ ] N Active and alert
- [ ] Y [ ] N Clear eyes (except when shedding)
- [ ] Y [ ] N Eats regularly
- [ ] Y [ ] N Good body composition
- [ ] Y [ ] N Healthy, supple, smooth skin
- [ ] Y [ ] N Regularly sheds skin in one complete piece
- [ ] Y [ ] N Free of mites and ticks

NOTES:

HIGHLIGHT OF THE WEEK:

DAILY CHECKLIST

Activity	WEEK OF

	SUN	MON	TUE	WED	THU	FRI	SAT
Clean and refresh water bowl	☐	☐	☐	☐	☐	☐	☐
Check temperatures	☐	☐	☐	☐	☐	☐	☐
Check humidity	☐	☐	☐	☐	☐	☐	☐
Spot clean any waste	☐	☐	☐	☐	☐	☐	☐
Remove any skin shed	☐	☐	☐	☐	☐	☐	☐
Visual inspect	☐	☐	☐	☐	☐	☐	☐

NOTES:

WEEKLY, MONTHLY CHECKLIST

WEEKLY ACTIVITY   DATE:

☐ Feed Snake

☐ Clean glass

☐ Top up substrate

☐ Clean any decorative wood, plants etc

☐ Physically inspect Snake

☐ Weigh and record

MONTHLY ACTIVITY   DATE:

☐ Remove and replace all substrate

HEALTH CHECKLIST   DATE:

☐Y ☐N Active and alert

☐Y ☐N Clear eyes (except when shedding)

☐Y ☐N Eats regularly

☐Y ☐N Good body composition

☐Y ☐N Healthy, supple, smooth skin

☐Y ☐N Regularly sheds skin in one complete piece

☐Y ☐N Free of mites and ticks

NOTES:

HIGHLIGHT OF THE WEEK:

DAILY CHECKLIST

Activity	WEEK OF						
	SUN	MON	TUE	WED	THU	FRI	SAT
Clean and refresh water bowl	☐	☐	☐	☐	☐	☐	☐
Check temperatures	☐	☐	☐	☐	☐	☐	☐
Check humidity	☐	☐	☐	☐	☐	☐	☐
Spot clean any waste	☐	☐	☐	☐	☐	☐	☐
Remove any skin shed	☐	☐	☐	☐	☐	☐	☐
Visual inspect	☐	☐	☐	☐	☐	☐	☐

NOTES:

WEEKLY, MONTHLY CHECKLIST

WEEKLY ACTIVITY   DATE:

- [ ] Feed Snake
- [ ] Clean glass
- [ ] Top up substrate
- [ ] Clean any decorative wood, plants etc
- [ ] Physically inspect Snake
- [ ] Weigh and record

MONTHLY ACTIVITY   DATE:

- [ ] Remove and replace all substrate

HEALTH CHECKLIST   DATE:

- [ ] Y [ ] N Active and alert
- [ ] Y [ ] N Clear eyes (except when shedding)
- [ ] Y [ ] N Eats regularly
- [ ] Y [ ] N Good body composition
- [ ] Y [ ] N Healthy, supple, smooth skin
- [ ] Y [ ] N Regularly sheds skin in one complete piece
- [ ] Y [ ] N Free of mites and ticks

NOTES:

HIGHLIGHT OF THE WEEK:

DAILY CHECKLIST

Activity	WEEK OF						
	SUN	MON	TUE	WED	THU	FRI	SAT
Clean and refresh water bowl	☐	☐	☐	☐	☐	☐	☐
Check temperatures	☐	☐	☐	☐	☐	☐	☐
Check humidity	☐	☐	☐	☐	☐	☐	☐
Spot clean any waste	☐	☐	☐	☐	☐	☐	☐
Remove any skin shed	☐	☐	☐	☐	☐	☐	☐
Visual inspect	☐	☐	☐	☐	☐	☐	☐

NOTES:

WEEKLY, MONTHLY CHECKLIST

WEEKLY ACTIVITY   DATE:

- [ ] Feed Snake
- [ ] Clean glass
- [ ] Top up substrate
- [ ] Clean any decorative wood, plants etc
- [ ] Physically inspect Snake
- [ ] Weigh and record

MONTHLY ACTIVITY   DATE:

- [ ] Remove and replace all substrate

HEALTH CHECKLIST   DATE:

- [ ] Y [ ] N Active and alert
- [ ] Y [ ] N Clear eyes (except when shedding)
- [ ] Y [ ] N Eats regularly
- [ ] Y [ ] N Good body composition
- [ ] Y [ ] N Healthy, supple, smooth skin
- [ ] Y [ ] N Regularly sheds skin in one complete piece
- [ ] Y [ ] N Free of mites and ticks

NOTES:

HIGHLIGHT OF THE WEEK:

DAILY CHECKLIST

Activity	WEEK OF						
	SUN	MON	TUE	WED	THU	FRI	SAT
Clean and refresh water bowl	☐	☐	☐	☐	☐	☐	☐
Check temperatures	☐	☐	☐	☐	☐	☐	☐
Check humidity	☐	☐	☐	☐	☐	☐	☐
Spot clean any waste	☐	☐	☐	☐	☐	☐	☐
Remove any skin shed	☐	☐	☐	☐	☐	☐	☐
Visual inspect	☐	☐	☐	☐	☐	☐	☐

NOTES:

WEEKLY, MONTHLY CHECKLIST

WEEKLY ACTIVITY   DATE:

- [ ] Feed Snake
- [ ] Clean glass
- [ ] Top up substrate
- [ ] Clean any decorative wood, plants etc
- [ ] Physically inspect Snake
- [ ] Weigh and record

MONTHLY ACTIVITY   DATE:

- [ ] Remove and replace all substrate

HEALTH CHECKLIST   DATE:

- Y / N   Active and alert
- Y / N   Clear eyes (except when shedding)
- Y / N   Eats regularly
- Y / N   Good body composition
- Y / N   Healthy, supple, smooth skin
- Y / N   Regularly sheds skin in one complete piece
- Y / N   Free of mites and ticks

NOTES:

HIGHLIGHT OF THE WEEK:

DAILY CHECKLIST

Activity	WEEK OF							
		SUN	MON	TUE	WED	THU	FRI	SAT
Clean and refresh water bowl		☐	☐	☐	☐	☐	☐	☐
Check temperatures		☐	☐	☐	☐	☐	☐	☐
Check humidity		☐	☐	☐	☐	☐	☐	☐
Spot clean any waste		☐	☐	☐	☐	☐	☐	☐
Remove any skin shed		☐	☐	☐	☐	☐	☐	☐
Visual inspect		☐	☐	☐	☐	☐	☐	☐

NOTES:

WEEKLY, MONTHLY CHECKLIST

WEEKLY ACTIVITY   DATE:

- ☐ Feed Snake
- ☐ Clean glass
- ☐ Top up substrate
- ☐ Clean any decorative wood, plants etc
- ☐ Physically inspect Snake
- ☐ Weigh and record

MONTHLY ACTIVITY   DATE:

- ☐ Remove and replace all substrate

HEALTH CHECKLIST   DATE:

- ☐ Y ☐ N Active and alert
- ☐ Y ☐ N Clear eyes (except when shedding)
- ☐ Y ☐ N Eats regularly
- ☐ Y ☐ N Good body composition
- ☐ Y ☐ N Healthy, supple, smooth skin
- ☐ Y ☐ N Regularly sheds skin in one complete piece
- ☐ Y ☐ N Free of mites and ticks

NOTES:

HIGHLIGHT OF THE WEEK:

DAILY CHECKLIST

Activity	WEEK OF						
	SUN	MON	TUE	WED	THU	FRI	SAT
Clean and refresh water bowl	☐	☐	☐	☐	☐	☐	☐
Check temperatures	☐	☐	☐	☐	☐	☐	☐
Check humidity	☐	☐	☐	☐	☐	☐	☐
Spot clean any waste	☐	☐	☐	☐	☐	☐	☐
Remove any skin shed	☐	☐	☐	☐	☐	☐	☐
Visual inspect	☐	☐	☐	☐	☐	☐	☐

NOTES:

WEEKLY, MONTHLY CHECKLIST

WEEKLY ACTIVITY   DATE: [ ]

- [ ] Feed Snake [ ]
- [ ] Clean glass
- [ ] Top up substrate
- [ ] Clean any decorative wood, plants etc
- [ ] Physically inspect Snake
- [ ] Weigh and record

[ ]

MONTHLY ACTIVITY   DATE: [ ]

- [ ] Remove and replace all substrate

HEALTH CHECKLIST   DATE: [ ]

- [Y] [N] Active and alert
- [Y] [N] Clear eyes (except when shedding)
- [Y] [N] Eats regularly
- [Y] [N] Good body composition
- [Y] [N] Healthy, supple, smooth skin
- [Y] [N] Regularly sheds skin in one complete piece
- [Y] [N] Free of mites and ticks

NOTES:

HIGHLIGHT OF THE WEEK:

DAILY CHECKLIST

Activity	WEEK OF						
	SUN	MON	TUE	WED	THU	FRI	SAT
Clean and refresh water bowl	☐	☐	☐	☐	☐	☐	☐
Check temperatures	☐	☐	☐	☐	☐	☐	☐
Check humidity	☐	☐	☐	☐	☐	☐	☐
Spot clean any waste	☐	☐	☐	☐	☐	☐	☐
Remove any skin shed	☐	☐	☐	☐	☐	☐	☐
Visual inspect	☐	☐	☐	☐	☐	☐	☐

NOTES:

WEEKLY, MONTHLY CHECKLIST

WEEKLY ACTIVITY   DATE:

- [ ] Feed Snake
- [ ] Clean glass
- [ ] Top up substrate
- [ ] Clean any decorative wood, plants etc
- [ ] Physically inspect Snake
- [ ] Weigh and record

MONTHLY ACTIVITY   DATE:

- [ ] Remove and replace all substrate

HEALTH CHECKLIST   DATE:

Y	N	
☐	☐	Active and alert
☐	☐	Clear eyes (except when shedding)
☐	☐	Eats regularly
☐	☐	Good body composition
☐	☐	Healthy, supple, smooth skin
☐	☐	Regularly sheds skin in one complete piece
☐	☐	Free of mites and ticks

NOTES:

HIGHLIGHT OF THE WEEK:

DAILY CHECKLIST

Activity	WEEK OF						
	SUN	MON	TUE	WED	THU	FRI	SAT
Clean and refresh water bowl	☐	☐	☐	☐	☐	☐	☐
Check temperatures	☐	☐	☐	☐	☐	☐	☐
Check humidity	☐	☐	☐	☐	☐	☐	☐
Spot clean any waste	☐	☐	☐	☐	☐	☐	☐
Remove any skin shed	☐	☐	☐	☐	☐	☐	☐
Visual inspect	☐	☐	☐	☐	☐	☐	☐

NOTES:

WEEKLY, MONTHLY CHECKLIST

WEEKLY ACTIVITY DATE: _____

☐ Feed Snake _____

☐ Clean glass

☐ Top up substrate

☐ Clean any decorative wood, plants etc

☐ Physically inspect Snake

☐ Weigh and record

_____

MONTHLY ACTIVITY DATE: _____

☐ Remove and replace all substrate

HEALTH CHECKLIST DATE: _____

☐Y ☐N Active and alert

☐Y ☐N Clear eyes (except when shedding)

☐Y ☐N Eats regularly

☐Y ☐N Good body composition

☐Y ☐N Healthy, supple, smooth skin

☐Y ☐N Regularly sheds skin in one complete piece

☐Y ☐N Free of mites and ticks

NOTES:

HIGHLIGHT OF THE WEEK:

DAILY CHECKLIST

Activity	WEEK OF	SUN	MON	TUE	WED	THU	FRI	SAT
Clean and refresh water bowl		☐	☐	☐	☐	☐	☐	☐
Check temperatures		☐	☐	☐	☐	☐	☐	☐
Check humidity		☐	☐	☐	☐	☐	☐	☐
Spot clean any waste		☐	☐	☐	☐	☐	☐	☐
Remove any skin shed		☐	☐	☐	☐	☐	☐	☐
Visual inspect		☐	☐	☐	☐	☐	☐	☐

NOTES:

WEEKLY, MONTHLY CHECKLIST

WEEKLY ACTIVITY   DATE:

- [ ] Feed Snake
- [ ] Clean glass
- [ ] Top up substrate
- [ ] Clean any decorative wood, plants etc
- [ ] Physically inspect Snake
- [ ] Weigh and record

MONTHLY ACTIVITY   DATE:

- [ ] Remove and replace all substrate

HEALTH CHECKLIST   DATE:

- Y N Active and alert
- Y N Clear eyes (except when shedding)
- Y N Eats regularly
- Y N Good body composition
- Y N Healthy, supple, smooth skin
- Y N Regularly sheds skin in one complete piece
- Y N Free of mites and ticks

NOTES:

HIGHLIGHT OF THE WEEK:

Activity	WEEK OF						
	SUN	MON	TUE	WED	THU	FRI	SAT
Clean and refresh water bowl	☐	☐	☐	☐	☐	☐	☐
Check temperatures	☐	☐	☐	☐	☐	☐	☐
Check humidity	☐	☐	☐	☐	☐	☐	☐
Spot clean any waste	☐	☐	☐	☐	☐	☐	☐
Remove any skin shed	☐	☐	☐	☐	☐	☐	☐
Visual inspect	☐	☐	☐	☐	☐	☐	☐

NOTES:

WEEKLY, MONTHLY CHECKLIST

WEEKLY ACTIVITY   DATE:

- [ ] Feed Snake
- [ ] Clean glass
- [ ] Top up substrate
- [ ] Clean any decorative wood, plants etc
- [ ] Physically inspect Snake
- [ ] Weigh and record

MONTHLY ACTIVITY   DATE:

- [ ] Remove and replace all substrate

HEALTH CHECKLIST   DATE:

- [Y] [N] Active and alert
- [Y] [N] Clear eyes (except when shedding)
- [Y] [N] Eats regularly
- [Y] [N] Good body composition
- [Y] [N] Healthy, supple, smooth skin
- [Y] [N] Regularly sheds skin in one complete piece
- [Y] [N] Free of mites and ticks

NOTES:

HIGHLIGHT OF THE WEEK:

DAILY CHECKLIST

📅 Activity	WEEK OF						
	SUN	MON	TUE	WED	THU	FRI	SAT
Clean and refresh water bowl	☐	☐	☐	☐	☐	☐	☐
Check temperatures	☐	☐	☐	☐	☐	☐	☐
Check humidity	☐	☐	☐	☐	☐	☐	☐
Spot clean any waste	☐	☐	☐	☐	☐	☐	☐
Remove any skin shed	☐	☐	☐	☐	☐	☐	☐
Visual inspect	☐	☐	☐	☐	☐	☐	☐

NOTES:

WEEKLY, MONTHLY CHECKLIST

WEEKLY ACTIVITY   DATE:

- [ ] Feed Snake
- [ ] Clean glass
- [ ] Top up substrate
- [ ] Clean any decorative wood, plants etc
- [ ] Physically inspect Snake
- [ ] Weigh and record

MONTHLY ACTIVITY   DATE:

- [ ] Remove and replace all substrate

HEALTH CHECKLIST   DATE:

- [Y] [N] Active and alert
- [Y] [N] Clear eyes (except when shedding)
- [Y] [N] Eats regularly
- [Y] [N] Good body composition
- [Y] [N] Healthy, supple, smooth skin
- [Y] [N] Regularly sheds skin in one complete piece
- [Y] [N] Free of mites and ticks

NOTES:

HIGHLIGHT OF THE WEEK:

DAILY CHECKLIST

Activity	WEEK OF						
	SUN	MON	TUE	WED	THU	FRI	SAT
Clean and refresh water bowl	☐	☐	☐	☐	☐	☐	☐
Check temperatures	☐	☐	☐	☐	☐	☐	☐
Check humidity	☐	☐	☐	☐	☐	☐	☐
Spot clean any waste	☐	☐	☐	☐	☐	☐	☐
Remove any skin shed	☐	☐	☐	☐	☐	☐	☐
Visual inspect	☐	☐	☐	☐	☐	☐	☐

NOTES:

WEEKLY, MONTHLY CHECKLIST

WEEKLY ACTIVITY　　DATE: _____

- ☐ Feed Snake _____
- ☐ Clean glass
- ☐ Top up substrate
- ☐ Clean any decorative wood, plants etc
- ☐ Physically inspect Snake
- ☐ Weigh and record

_____

MONTHLY ACTIVITY　　DATE: _____

- ☐ Remove and replace all substrate

HEALTH CHECKLIST　　DATE: _____

- ☐Y ☐N Active and alert
- ☐Y ☐N Clear eyes (except when shedding)
- ☐Y ☐N Eats regularly
- ☐Y ☐N Good body composition
- ☐Y ☐N Healthy, supple, smooth skin
- ☐Y ☐N Regularly sheds skin in one complete piece
- ☐Y ☐N Free of mites and ticks

NOTES:

HIGHLIGHT OF THE WEEK:

DAILY CHECKLIST

Activity	WEEK OF						
	SUN	MON	TUE	WED	THU	FRI	SAT
Clean and refresh water bowl	☐	☐	☐	☐	☐	☐	☐
Check temperatures	☐	☐	☐	☐	☐	☐	☐
Check humidity	☐	☐	☐	☐	☐	☐	☐
Spot clean any waste	☐	☐	☐	☐	☐	☐	☐
Remove any skin shed	☐	☐	☐	☐	☐	☐	☐
Visual inspect	☐	☐	☐	☐	☐	☐	☐

NOTES:

WEEKLY, MONTHLY CHECKLIST

WEEKLY ACTIVITY   DATE:

- [ ] Feed Snake
- [ ] Clean glass
- [ ] Top up substrate
- [ ] Clean any decorative wood, plants etc
- [ ] Physically inspect Snake
- [ ] Weigh and record

MONTHLY ACTIVITY   DATE:

- [ ] Remove and replace all substrate

HEALTH CHECKLIST   DATE:

- [ ] Y [ ] N Active and alert
- [ ] Y [ ] N Clear eyes (except when shedding)
- [ ] Y [ ] N Eats regularly
- [ ] Y [ ] N Good body composition
- [ ] Y [ ] N Healthy, supple, smooth skin
- [ ] Y [ ] N Regularly sheds skin in one complete piece
- [ ] Y [ ] N Free of mites and ticks

NOTES:

HIGHLIGHT OF THE WEEK:

DAILY CHECKLIST

📅 **Activity**

WEEK OF _____

	SUN	MON	TUE	WED	THU	FRI	SAT
Clean and refresh water bowl	☐	☐	☐	☐	☐	☐	☐
Check temperatures	☐	☐	☐	☐	☐	☐	☐
Check humidity	☐	☐	☐	☐	☐	☐	☐
Spot clean any waste	☐	☐	☐	☐	☐	☐	☐
Remove any skin shed	☐	☐	☐	☐	☐	☐	☐
Visual inspect	☐	☐	☐	☐	☐	☐	☐

NOTES:

WEEKLY, MONTHLY CHECKLIST

WEEKLY ACTIVITY   DATE: [   ]

- ☐ Feed Snake [   ]
- ☐ Clean glass
- ☐ Top up substrate
- ☐ Clean any decorative wood, plants etc
- ☐ Physically inspect Snake
- ☐ Weigh and record

[   ]

MONTHLY ACTIVITY   DATE: [   ]

- ☐ Remove and replace all substrate

HEALTH CHECKLIST   DATE: [   ]

- ☐Y ☐N Active and alert
- ☐Y ☐N Clear eyes (except when shedding)
- ☐Y ☐N Eats regularly
- ☐Y ☐N Good body composition
- ☐Y ☐N Healthy, supple, smooth skin
- ☐Y ☐N Regularly sheds skin in one complete piece
- ☐Y ☐N Free of mites and ticks

NOTES:

HIGHLIGHT OF THE WEEK:

DAILY CHECKLIST

Activity	WEEK OF						
	SUN	MON	TUE	WED	THU	FRI	SAT
Clean and refresh water bowl	☐	☐	☐	☐	☐	☐	☐
Check temperatures	☐	☐	☐	☐	☐	☐	☐
Check humidity	☐	☐	☐	☐	☐	☐	☐
Spot clean any waste	☐	☐	☐	☐	☐	☐	☐
Remove any skin shed	☐	☐	☐	☐	☐	☐	☐
Visual inspect	☐	☐	☐	☐	☐	☐	☐

NOTES:

WEEKLY, MONTHLY CHECKLIST

WEEKLY ACTIVITY   DATE:

- [ ] Feed Snake
- [ ] Clean glass
- [ ] Top up substrate
- [ ] Clean any decorative wood, plants etc
- [ ] Physically inspect Snake
- [ ] Weigh and record

MONTHLY ACTIVITY   DATE:

- [ ] Remove and replace all substrate

HEALTH CHECKLIST   DATE:

- [ ] Y [ ] N Active and alert
- [ ] Y [ ] N Clear eyes (except when shedding)
- [ ] Y [ ] N Eats regularly
- [ ] Y [ ] N Good body composition
- [ ] Y [ ] N Healthy, supple, smooth skin
- [ ] Y [ ] N Regularly sheds skin in one complete piece
- [ ] Y [ ] N Free of mites and ticks

NOTES:

HIGHLIGHT OF THE WEEK:

DAILY CHECKLIST

Activity	WEEK OF						
	SUN	MON	TUE	WED	THU	FRI	SAT
Clean and refresh water bowl	☐	☐	☐	☐	☐	☐	☐
Check temperatures	☐	☐	☐	☐	☐	☐	☐
Check humidity	☐	☐	☐	☐	☐	☐	☐
Spot clean any waste	☐	☐	☐	☐	☐	☐	☐
Remove any skin shed	☐	☐	☐	☐	☐	☐	☐
Visual inspect	☐	☐	☐	☐	☐	☐	☐

NOTES:

WEEKLY, MONTHLY CHECKLIST

WEEKLY ACTIVITY DATE:

- [ ] Feed Snake
- [ ] Clean glass
- [ ] Top up substrate
- [ ] Clean any decorative wood, plants etc
- [ ] Physically inspect Snake
- [ ] Weigh and record

MONTHLY ACTIVITY DATE:

- [ ] Remove and replace all substrate

HEALTH CHECKLIST DATE:

- Y / N Active and alert
- Y / N Clear eyes (except when shedding)
- Y / N Eats regularly
- Y / N Good body composition
- Y / N Healthy, supple, smooth skin
- Y / N Regularly sheds skin in one complete piece
- Y / N Free of mites and ticks

NOTES:

HIGHLIGHT OF THE WEEK:

DAILY CHECKLIST

Activity	WEEK OF						
	SUN	MON	TUE	WED	THU	FRI	SAT
Clean and refresh water bowl	☐	☐	☐	☐	☐	☐	☐
Check temperatures	☐	☐	☐	☐	☐	☐	☐
Check humidity	☐	☐	☐	☐	☐	☐	☐
Spot clean any waste	☐	☐	☐	☐	☐	☐	☐
Remove any skin shed	☐	☐	☐	☐	☐	☐	☐
Visual inspect	☐	☐	☐	☐	☐	☐	☐

NOTES:

WEEKLY, MONTHLY CHECKLIST

WEEKLY ACTIVITY   DATE:

- [ ] Feed Snake
- [ ] Clean glass
- [ ] Top up substrate
- [ ] Clean any decorative wood, plants etc
- [ ] Physically inspect Snake
- [ ] Weigh and record

MONTHLY ACTIVITY   DATE:

- [ ] Remove and replace all substrate

HEALTH CHECKLIST   DATE:

- [Y] [N] Active and alert
- [Y] [N] Clear eyes (except when shedding)
- [Y] [N] Eats regularly
- [Y] [N] Good body composition
- [Y] [N] Healthy, supple, smooth skin
- [Y] [N] Regularly sheds skin in one complete piece
- [Y] [N] Free of mites and ticks

NOTES:

HIGHLIGHT OF THE WEEK:

DAILY CHECKLIST

Activity	WEEK OF						
	SUN	MON	TUE	WED	THU	FRI	SAT
Clean and refresh water bowl	☐	☐	☐	☐	☐	☐	☐
Check temperatures	☐	☐	☐	☐	☐	☐	☐
Check humidity	☐	☐	☐	☐	☐	☐	☐
Spot clean any waste	☐	☐	☐	☐	☐	☐	☐
Remove any skin shed	☐	☐	☐	☐	☐	☐	☐
Visual inspect	☐	☐	☐	☐	☐	☐	☐

NOTES:

WEEKLY, MONTHLY CHECKLIST

WEEKLY ACTIVITY   DATE: _____

- ☐ Feed Snake _____
- ☐ Clean glass
- ☐ Top up substrate
- ☐ Clean any decorative wood, plants etc
- ☐ Physically inspect Snake
- ☐ Weigh and record

_____

MONTHLY ACTIVITY   DATE: _____

- ☐ Remove and replace all substrate

HEALTH CHECKLIST   DATE: _____

- ☐Y ☐N Active and alert
- ☐Y ☐N Clear eyes (except when shedding)
- ☐Y ☐N Eats regularly
- ☐Y ☐N Good body composition
- ☐Y ☐N Healthy, supple, smooth skin
- ☐Y ☐N Regularly sheds skin in one complete piece
- ☐Y ☐N Free of mites and ticks

NOTES:

HIGHLIGHT OF THE WEEK:

DAILY CHECKLIST

Activity	WEEK OF						
	SUN	MON	TUE	WED	THU	FRI	SAT
Clean and refresh water bowl	☐	☐	☐	☐	☐	☐	☐
Check temperatures	☐	☐	☐	☐	☐	☐	☐
Check humidity	☐	☐	☐	☐	☐	☐	☐
Spot clean any waste	☐	☐	☐	☐	☐	☐	☐
Remove any skin shed	☐	☐	☐	☐	☐	☐	☐
Visual inspect	☐	☐	☐	☐	☐	☐	☐

NOTES:

WEEKLY, MONTHLY CHECKLIST

WEEKLY ACTIVITY   DATE: [   ]

- [ ] Feed Snake [   ]
- [ ] Clean glass
- [ ] Top up substrate
- [ ] Clean any decorative wood, plants etc
- [ ] Physically inspect Snake
- [ ] Weigh and record

[   ]

MONTHLY ACTIVITY   DATE: [   ]

- [ ] Remove and replace all substrate

HEALTH CHECKLIST   DATE: [   ]

- Y ☐ N ☐ Active and alert
- Y ☐ N ☐ Clear eyes (except when shedding)
- Y ☐ N ☐ Eats regularly
- Y ☐ N ☐ Good body composition
- Y ☐ N ☐ Healthy, supple, smooth skin
- Y ☐ N ☐ Regularly sheds skin in one complete piece
- Y ☐ N ☐ Free of mites and ticks

NOTES:

HIGHLIGHT OF THE WEEK:

DAILY CHECKLIST

Activity	WEEK OF	SUN	MON	TUE	WED	THU	FRI	SAT
Clean and refresh water bowl		☐	☐	☐	☐	☐	☐	☐
Check temperatures		☐	☐	☐	☐	☐	☐	☐
Check humidity		☐	☐	☐	☐	☐	☐	☐
Spot clean any waste		☐	☐	☐	☐	☐	☐	☐
Remove any skin shed		☐	☐	☐	☐	☐	☐	☐
Visual inspect		☐	☐	☐	☐	☐	☐	☐

NOTES:

WEEKLY, MONTHLY CHECKLIST

WEEKLY ACTIVITY — DATE:

- ☐ Feed Snake
- ☐ Clean glass
- ☐ Top up substrate
- ☐ Clean any decorative wood, plants etc
- ☐ Physically inspect Snake
- ☐ Weigh and record

MONTHLY ACTIVITY — DATE:

- ☐ Remove and replace all substrate

HEALTH CHECKLIST — DATE:

- ☐ Y ☐ N Active and alert
- ☐ Y ☐ N Clear eyes (except when shedding)
- ☐ Y ☐ N Eats regularly
- ☐ Y ☐ N Good body composition
- ☐ Y ☐ N Healthy, supple, smooth skin
- ☐ Y ☐ N Regularly sheds skin in one complete piece
- ☐ Y ☐ N Free of mites and ticks

NOTES:

HIGHLIGHT OF THE WEEK:

DAILY CHECKLIST

Activity	WEEK OF						
	SUN	MON	TUE	WED	THU	FRI	SAT
Clean and refresh water bowl	☐	☐	☐	☐	☐	☐	☐
Check temperatures	☐	☐	☐	☐	☐	☐	☐
Check humidity	☐	☐	☐	☐	☐	☐	☐
Spot clean any waste	☐	☐	☐	☐	☐	☐	☐
Remove any skin shed	☐	☐	☐	☐	☐	☐	☐
Visual inspect	☐	☐	☐	☐	☐	☐	☐

NOTES:

WEEKLY, MONTHLY CHECKLIST

WEEKLY ACTIVITY   DATE: ____

- [ ] Feed Snake ____
- [ ] Clean glass
- [ ] Top up substrate
- [ ] Clean any decorative wood, plants etc
- [ ] Physically inspect Snake
- [ ] Weigh and record

____

MONTHLY ACTIVITY   DATE: ____

- [ ] Remove and replace all substrate

HEALTH CHECKLIST   DATE: ____

- [Y] [N] Active and alert
- [Y] [N] Clear eyes (except when shedding)
- [Y] [N] Eats regularly
- [Y] [N] Good body composition
- [Y] [N] Healthy, supple, smooth skin
- [Y] [N] Regularly sheds skin in one complete piece
- [Y] [N] Free of mites and ticks

NOTES:

HIGHLIGHT OF THE WEEK:

DAILY CHECKLIST

Activity	WEEK OF						
	SUN	MON	TUE	WED	THU	FRI	SAT
Clean and refresh water bowl	☐	☐	☐	☐	☐	☐	☐
Check temperatures	☐	☐	☐	☐	☐	☐	☐
Check humidity	☐	☐	☐	☐	☐	☐	☐
Spot clean any waste	☐	☐	☐	☐	☐	☐	☐
Remove any skin shed	☐	☐	☐	☐	☐	☐	☐
Visual inspect	☐	☐	☐	☐	☐	☐	☐

NOTES:

WEEKLY, MONTHLY CHECKLIST

WEEKLY ACTIVITY   DATE:

- [ ] Feed Snake
- [ ] Clean glass
- [ ] Top up substrate
- [ ] Clean any decorative wood, plants etc
- [ ] Physically inspect Snake
- [ ] Weigh and record

MONTHLY ACTIVITY   DATE:

- [ ] Remove and replace all substrate

HEALTH CHECKLIST   DATE:

- Y N Active and alert
- Y N Clear eyes (except when shedding)
- Y N Eats regularly
- Y N Good body composition
- Y N Healthy, supple, smooth skin
- Y N Regularly sheds skin in one complete piece
- Y N Free of mites and ticks

NOTES:

HIGHLIGHT OF THE WEEK:

DAILY CHECKLIST

Activity	WEEK OF
	SUN MON TUE WED THU FRI SAT
Clean and refresh water bowl	☐ ☐ ☐ ☐ ☐ ☐ ☐
Check temperatures	☐ ☐ ☐ ☐ ☐ ☐ ☐
Check humidity	☐ ☐ ☐ ☐ ☐ ☐ ☐
Spot clean any waste	☐ ☐ ☐ ☐ ☐ ☐ ☐
Remove any skin shed	☐ ☐ ☐ ☐ ☐ ☐ ☐
Visual inspect	☐ ☐ ☐ ☐ ☐ ☐ ☐

NOTES:

WEEKLY, MONTHLY CHECKLIST

WEEKLY ACTIVITY   DATE:

☐ Feed Snake

☐ Clean glass

☐ Top up substrate

☐ Clean any decorative wood, plants etc

☐ Physically inspect Snake

☐ Weigh and record

MONTHLY ACTIVITY   DATE:

☐ Remove and replace all substrate

HEALTH CHECKLIST   DATE:

☐Y ☐N Active and alert

☐Y ☐N Clear eyes (except when shedding)

☐Y ☐N Eats regularly

☐Y ☐N Good body composition

☐Y ☐N Healthy, supple, smooth skin

☐Y ☐N Regularly sheds skin in one complete piece

☐Y ☐N Free of mites and ticks

NOTES:

HIGHLIGHT OF THE WEEK:

DAILY CHECKLIST

Activity	WEEK OF	SUN	MON	TUE	WED	THU	FRI	SAT
Clean and refresh water bowl		☐	☐	☐	☐	☐	☐	☐
Check temperatures		☐	☐	☐	☐	☐	☐	☐
Check humidity		☐	☐	☐	☐	☐	☐	☐
Spot clean any waste		☐	☐	☐	☐	☐	☐	☐
Remove any skin shed		☐	☐	☐	☐	☐	☐	☐
Visual inspect		☐	☐	☐	☐	☐	☐	☐

NOTES:

WEEKLY, MONTHLY CHECKLIST

WEEKLY ACTIVITY   DATE:

- [ ] Feed Snake
- [ ] Clean glass
- [ ] Top up substrate
- [ ] Clean any decorative wood, plants etc
- [ ] Physically inspect Snake
- [ ] Weigh and record

MONTHLY ACTIVITY   DATE:

- [ ] Remove and replace all substrate

HEALTH CHECKLIST   DATE:

- [ ] Y [ ] N Active and alert
- [ ] Y [ ] N Clear eyes (except when shedding)
- [ ] Y [ ] N Eats regularly
- [ ] Y [ ] N Good body composition
- [ ] Y [ ] N Healthy, supple, smooth skin
- [ ] Y [ ] N Regularly sheds skin in one complete piece
- [ ] Y [ ] N Free of mites and ticks

NOTES:

HIGHLIGHT OF THE WEEK:

Activity	WEEK OF	SUN	MON	TUE	WED	THU	FRI	SAT
Clean and refresh water bowl		☐	☐	☐	☐	☐	☐	☐
Check temperatures		☐	☐	☐	☐	☐	☐	☐
Check humidity		☐	☐	☐	☐	☐	☐	☐
Spot clean any waste		☐	☐	☐	☐	☐	☐	☐
Remove any skin shed		☐	☐	☐	☐	☐	☐	☐
Visual inspect		☐	☐	☐	☐	☐	☐	☐

NOTES:

WEEKLY, MONTHLY CHECKLIST

WEEKLY ACTIVITY   DATE: [   ]

- [ ] Feed Snake [   ]
- [ ] Clean glass
- [ ] Top up substrate
- [ ] Clean any decorative wood, plants etc
- [ ] Physically inspect Snake
- [ ] Weigh and record

[   ]

MONTHLY ACTIVITY   DATE: [   ]

- [ ] Remove and replace all substrate

HEALTH CHECKLIST   DATE: [   ]

Y	N	
☐	☐	Active and alert
☐	☐	Clear eyes (except when shedding)
☐	☐	Eats regularly
☐	☐	Good body composition
☐	☐	Healthy, supple, smooth skin
☐	☐	Regularly sheds skin in one complete piece
☐	☐	Free of mites and ticks

NOTES:

HIGHLIGHT OF THE WEEK:

DAILY CHECKLIST

Activity	WEEK OF						
	SUN	MON	TUE	WED	THU	FRI	SAT
Clean and refresh water bowl	☐	☐	☐	☐	☐	☐	☐
Check temperatures	☐	☐	☐	☐	☐	☐	☐
Check humidity	☐	☐	☐	☐	☐	☐	☐
Spot clean any waste	☐	☐	☐	☐	☐	☐	☐
Remove any skin shed	☐	☐	☐	☐	☐	☐	☐
Visual inspect	☐	☐	☐	☐	☐	☐	☐

NOTES:

WEEKLY, MONTHLY CHECKLIST

WEEKLY ACTIVITY   DATE: [   ]

☐ Feed Snake [   ]

☐ Clean glass

☐ Top up substrate

☐ Clean any decorative wood, plants etc

☐ Physically inspect Snake

☐ Weigh and record

[   ]

MONTHLY ACTIVITY   DATE: [   ]

☐ Remove and replace all substrate

HEALTH CHECKLIST   DATE: [   ]

☐Y ☐N Active and alert

☐Y ☐N Clear eyes (except when shedding)

☐Y ☐N Eats regularly

☐Y ☐N Good body composition

☐Y ☐N Healthy, supple, smooth skin

☐Y ☐N Regularly sheds skin in one complete piece

☐Y ☐N Free of mites and ticks

NOTES:

HIGHLIGHT OF THE WEEK:

DAILY CHECKLIST

Activity	WEEK OF						
	SUN	MON	TUE	WED	THU	FRI	SAT
Clean and refresh water bowl	☐	☐	☐	☐	☐	☐	☐
Check temperatures	☐	☐	☐	☐	☐	☐	☐
Check humidity	☐	☐	☐	☐	☐	☐	☐
Spot clean any waste	☐	☐	☐	☐	☐	☐	☐
Remove any skin shed	☐	☐	☐	☐	☐	☐	☐
Visual inspect	☐	☐	☐	☐	☐	☐	☐

NOTES:

WEEKLY, MONTHLY CHECKLIST

WEEKLY ACTIVITY   DATE:

- [ ] Feed Snake
- [ ] Clean glass
- [ ] Top up substrate
- [ ] Clean any decorative wood, plants etc
- [ ] Physically inspect Snake
- [ ] Weigh and record

MONTHLY ACTIVITY   DATE:

- [ ] Remove and replace all substrate

HEALTH CHECKLIST   DATE:

- Y N Active and alert
- Y N Clear eyes (except when shedding)
- Y N Eats regularly
- Y N Good body composition
- Y N Healthy, supple, smooth skin
- Y N Regularly sheds skin in one complete piece
- Y N Free of mites and ticks

NOTES:

HIGHLIGHT OF THE WEEK:

DAILY CHECKLIST

Activity	WEEK OF						
	SUN	MON	TUE	WED	THU	FRI	SAT
Clean and refresh water bowl	☐	☐	☐	☐	☐	☐	☐
Check temperatures	☐	☐	☐	☐	☐	☐	☐
Check humidity	☐	☐	☐	☐	☐	☐	☐
Spot clean any waste	☐	☐	☐	☐	☐	☐	☐
Remove any skin shed	☐	☐	☐	☐	☐	☐	☐
Visual inspect	☐	☐	☐	☐	☐	☐	☐

NOTES:

WEEKLY, MONTHLY CHECKLIST

WEEKLY ACTIVITY   DATE: [   ]

- ☐ Feed Snake [   ]
- ☐ Clean glass
- ☐ Top up substrate
- ☐ Clean any decorative wood, plants etc
- ☐ Physically inspect Snake
- ☐ Weigh and record

[   ]

MONTHLY ACTIVITY   DATE: [   ]

- ☐ Remove and replace all substrate

HEALTH CHECKLIST   DATE: [   ]

- Y ☐ N ☐ Active and alert
- Y ☐ N ☐ Clear eyes (except when shedding)
- Y ☐ N ☐ Eats regularly
- Y ☐ N ☐ Good body composition
- Y ☐ N ☐ Healthy, supple, smooth skin
- Y ☐ N ☐ Regularly sheds skin in one complete piece
- Y ☐ N ☐ Free of mites and ticks

NOTES:

HIGHLIGHT OF THE WEEK:

DAILY CHECKLIST

Activity	WEEK OF						
	SUN	MON	TUE	WED	THU	FRI	SAT
Clean and refresh water bowl	☐	☐	☐	☐	☐	☐	☐
Check temperatures	☐	☐	☐	☐	☐	☐	☐
Check humidity	☐	☐	☐	☐	☐	☐	☐
Spot clean any waste	☐	☐	☐	☐	☐	☐	☐
Remove any skin shed	☐	☐	☐	☐	☐	☐	☐
Visual inspect	☐	☐	☐	☐	☐	☐	☐

NOTES:

WEEKLY, MONTHLY CHECKLIST

WEEKLY ACTIVITY   DATE: ☐

☐ Feed Snake ☐

☐ Clean glass

☐ Top up substrate

☐ Clean any decorative wood, plants etc

☐ Physically inspect Snake

☐ Weigh and record

☐

MONTHLY ACTIVITY   DATE: ☐

☐ Remove and replace all substrate

HEALTH CHECKLIST   DATE: ☐

☐Y ☐N Active and alert

☐Y ☐N Clear eyes (except when shedding)

☐Y ☐N Eats regularly

☐Y ☐N Good body composition

☐Y ☐N Healthy, supple, smooth skin

☐Y ☐N Regularly sheds skin in one complete piece

☐Y ☐N Free of mites and ticks

NOTES:

HIGHLIGHT OF THE WEEK:

DAILY CHECKLIST

Activity	WEEK OF						
	SUN	MON	TUE	WED	THU	FRI	SAT
Clean and refresh water bowl	☐	☐	☐	☐	☐	☐	☐
Check temperatures	☐	☐	☐	☐	☐	☐	☐
Check humidity	☐	☐	☐	☐	☐	☐	☐
Spot clean any waste	☐	☐	☐	☐	☐	☐	☐
Remove any skin shed	☐	☐	☐	☐	☐	☐	☐
Visual inspect	☐	☐	☐	☐	☐	☐	☐

NOTES:

WEEKLY, MONTHLY CHECKLIST

WEEKLY ACTIVITY   DATE:

- [ ] Feed Snake
- [ ] Clean glass
- [ ] Top up substrate
- [ ] Clean any decorative wood, plants etc
- [ ] Physically inspect Snake
- [ ] Weigh and record

MONTHLY ACTIVITY   DATE:

- [ ] Remove and replace all substrate

HEALTH CHECKLIST   DATE:

- [Y] [N] Active and alert
- [Y] [N] Clear eyes (except when shedding)
- [Y] [N] Eats regularly
- [Y] [N] Good body composition
- [Y] [N] Healthy, supple, smooth skin
- [Y] [N] Regularly sheds skin in one complete piece
- [Y] [N] Free of mites and ticks

NOTES:

HIGHLIGHT OF THE WEEK:

DAILY CHECKLIST

Activity	WEEK OF						
	SUN	MON	TUE	WED	THU	FRI	SAT
Clean and refresh water bowl	☐	☐	☐	☐	☐	☐	☐
Check temperatures	☐	☐	☐	☐	☐	☐	☐
Check humidity	☐	☐	☐	☐	☐	☐	☐
Spot clean any waste	☐	☐	☐	☐	☐	☐	☐
Remove any skin shed	☐	☐	☐	☐	☐	☐	☐
Visual inspect	☐	☐	☐	☐	☐	☐	☐

NOTES:

WEEKLY, MONTHLY CHECKLIST

WEEKLY ACTIVITY   DATE:

- ☐ Feed Snake
- ☐ Clean glass
- ☐ Top up substrate
- ☐ Clean any decorative wood, plants etc
- ☐ Physically inspect Snake
- ☐ Weigh and record

MONTHLY ACTIVITY   DATE:

- ☐ Remove and replace all substrate

HEALTH CHECKLIST   DATE:

- ☐Y ☐N Active and alert
- ☐Y ☐N Clear eyes (except when shedding)
- ☐Y ☐N Eats regularly
- ☐Y ☐N Good body composition
- ☐Y ☐N Healthy, supple, smooth skin
- ☐Y ☐N Regularly sheds skin in one complete piece
- ☐Y ☐N Free of mites and ticks

NOTES:

HIGHLIGHT OF THE WEEK:

DAILY CHECKLIST

Activity	WEEK OF						
	SUN	MON	TUE	WED	THU	FRI	SAT
Clean and refresh water bowl	☐	☐	☐	☐	☐	☐	☐
Check temperatures	☐	☐	☐	☐	☐	☐	☐
Check humidity	☐	☐	☐	☐	☐	☐	☐
Spot clean any waste	☐	☐	☐	☐	☐	☐	☐
Remove any skin shed	☐	☐	☐	☐	☐	☐	☐
Visual inspect	☐	☐	☐	☐	☐	☐	☐

NOTES:

WEEKLY, MONTHLY CHECKLIST

WEEKLY ACTIVITY   DATE: _____

- [ ] Feed Snake _____
- [ ] Clean glass
- [ ] Top up substrate
- [ ] Clean any decorative wood, plants etc
- [ ] Physically inspect Snake
- [ ] Weigh and record

_____

MONTHLY ACTIVITY   DATE: _____

- [ ] Remove and replace all substrate

HEALTH CHECKLIST   DATE: _____

Y	N	
☐	☐	Active and alert
☐	☐	Clear eyes (except when shedding)
☐	☐	Eats regularly
☐	☐	Good body composition
☐	☐	Healthy, supple, smooth skin
☐	☐	Regularly sheds skin in one complete piece
☐	☐	Free of mites and ticks

NOTES:

HIGHLIGHT OF THE WEEK:

DAILY CHECKLIST

Activity	WEEK OF							
	SUN	MON	TUE	WED	THU	FRI	SAT
Clean and refresh water bowl	☐	☐	☐	☐	☐	☐	☐
Check temperatures	☐	☐	☐	☐	☐	☐	☐
Check humidity	☐	☐	☐	☐	☐	☐	☐
Spot clean any waste	☐	☐	☐	☐	☐	☐	☐
Remove any skin shed	☐	☐	☐	☐	☐	☐	☐
Visual inspect	☐	☐	☐	☐	☐	☐	☐

NOTES:

WEEKLY, MONTHLY CHECKLIST

WEEKLY ACTIVITY   DATE: [   ]

- [ ] Feed Snake [   ]
- [ ] Clean glass
- [ ] Top up substrate
- [ ] Clean any decorative wood, plants etc
- [ ] Physically inspect Snake
- [ ] Weigh and record

[   ]

MONTHLY ACTIVITY   DATE: [   ]

- [ ] Remove and replace all substrate

HEALTH CHECKLIST   DATE: [   ]

- [Y] [N] Active and alert
- [Y] [N] Clear eyes (except when shedding)
- [Y] [N] Eats regularly
- [Y] [N] Good body composition
- [Y] [N] Healthy, supple, smooth skin
- [Y] [N] Regularly sheds skin in one complete piece
- [Y] [N] Free of mites and ticks

NOTES:

HIGHLIGHT OF THE WEEK:

MY PET
BALL PYTHON LOGBOOK